BY PETER DAVISON

BARN FEVER

Back Country by Thomas W. Nason

BARN FEVER

AND OTHER POEMS

PETER DAVISON

ATHENEUM *NEW YORK*

1981

The following poems appear through the courtesy of the
following periodicals:

AMERICAN SCHOLAR: *Untuned String, Fawn*
THE ATLANTIC: *The Sound of Wings, The Laughter of Women*
BOSTON MONTHLY: *Interval*
COUNTRY JOURNAL: *Barn Fever*
HARVARD MAGAZINE: *Satan in Goatskin*
HARPER'S: *My Lady the Lake*
HUDSON REVIEW: *Clinical Depression, The Clinic, Willing Her
to Live, Frozen Drought, The Householder,
After Winter Slaughtering, The Writing Lesson*
NEW ENGLAND REVIEW: *New Year's Eve, On Ithaca, Il Se Sauve,
Paradise as a Garden*
THE NEW YORKER: *The Ram Beneath the Barn*
PEQUOD: *Atmospheres*
POETRY: *July Meeting*
POETRY NORTHWEST: *The Transvestite's Dream*

Library of Congress Cataloging in Publication Data

Davison, Peter.
    Barn fever and other poems.

    I. Title.
PS3554.A94B3   811'.54 [B]   80-69364
ISBN 0-689-11126-6
ISBN 0-689-11163-0 (pbk.)

Published simultaneously in Canada by McClelland and Stewart Ltd
Manufactured by American Book–Stratford Press,
Saddle Brook, New Jersey
Designed by Harry Ford
First Edition

*The wood engraving by Thomas W. Nason is reproduced
with kind permission of Mrs. Nason.*

FOR JANE, WRITING

For over twenty years you have endowed me
with poems it seemed to me I had discovered,
and with nearly every stability
I knew enough to know.
Your laughter freckles the horizon,
aurora meridionalis.
You sit in a work chair
the way a heron stands—
motionless, gazing down at the paper.
Then, with the flicker of a smile,
you lean for the fish
with pencil or stammering key.

Gift: The act, right, or power of giving. *Webster*

What really interests me is whether God had any choice in the making of the universe.

Albert Einstein

CONTENTS

IV *MIXED BLESSINGS*

I

PASTURES AND MEADOWS

Gift: With respect to real estate, formerly, any form of alienation. *Webster*

A farm is such a carnival of birth and death,
there is no wonder it should frighten a child . . .
Yet these first fears, coming from things so
bound up with life, were probably good, and
a child could not grow up in a better place
than a farm; for at the heart of human civi-
lization is the byre, the barn, and the midden.

Edwin Muir, An Autobiography

THE RAM BENEATH THE BARN

Deep in the barn beneath foundation walls
the thick ram lies, his bent forefeet tucked under.

The droppings of a winter foul his straw,
but I dare no longer venture to his level
with grain, hay, water. I lower them to him
as to a tribe closed off by mountain snows.

He walks out into the sun, looks up at me,
his eyes expressionless as agates. He waits
for the moment of revenge. One day he may
catch me in a corner! Meanwhile, to prime his aim,
he taps his head and horns against the granite.

Of course when autumn comes he will again
curl up his lips into the sneer of lust
and leap his docile ewes, rolling their stupid
eyes as he does them his service—

but in this March we stare each other down,
two rams caught in a thicket by the horns.

INTERVAL

In the thick air of early September
mornings, crows call uninterrupted,
no competition. The whirr of katydids
keeps up an incessant thermograph
of sound, invisible orchestra
rising with light and heat,
falling with cold and dark,
to steal the place of songbirds in the spectrum.

In the trees squirrels scramble
to stuff their pouches
with a season of beech nuts.
In the garden they shinny
up sunflower stalks to keep
the black seeds from falling prey
to incoming winter birds.
Tomatoes enrich their sagging vines
like Christmas baubles.

Except for one abandoned chick
too slow or small to fly, lying broken
and dead beside the lawnmower,
the barn has emptied of swallows.

New piglets, just learning
the taste of man's food, skitter
away from the fence each time
a wagging dog approaches.
Geese roost in the shade.
Sheep munch stolidly whatever
green blades survive
as members of the yellow medley of grass.

On such days between
their summer jobs and school
the children sleep till noon,
clothes and towels swathing
the floor like serpents.
In the meadow a girl exercises
a long-barreled grey gelding
with patches on his rump
and a tail like a chieftain's whisk.
They canter together around and around the field.
Katydids lower their buzz.

Black leaves are scarcely moving
on the trees. Along the wires
and in the willow branches
a thousand tree swallows stir and twitter,
awaiting a signal
to set off for Yucatán.

LAMBKILL

(Sheep Laurel, kalmia angustifolia)

Yielding far more than we had ever sown—
lushness of fescue laced with grapevine
and poison ivy, raspberries loud with bees—
the land flowed with milkweed and honeysuckle
in surpluses that seemed to call for forage
by expansionist sheep. They had already munched
three pastures down to rugs. We felled and set
five dozen posts, strung a furlong of wire,
and set up gates to keep the sheep shut in.

At first they didn't like this newest pasture,
something about the wind, the angle of the sun,
marsh flies buzzing around their flipflop ears.
They slept burrowing their muzzles under each other.
Waking, they browsed their way through the inscrutable,
bawling out their wish for a view of level grass,
hungry for simplicity. They thrust heads
through the wiring of their fence to nibble lawn
that stretched out ahead like understanding
while cryptic stands of fodder rustled behind.

After three weeks of grazing, the meadow showed signs
of altering into pasture. The high grass dwindled.
Raspberries receded, poison ivy vanished.
Sheep trails stole a march across the ground.
We'd wondered whether a mere dozen animals
could clear out half an acre in a month,
and by the end of June it was nearly done.
On Sunday morning when I brought their grain
all but one sheep ran up at the clank
of the feeding pail. He, a six-month's ram,

stood oddly, head hanging, clearly sick.
An hour later he lay thrashing on his side
spasmodic by the galvanized water tub.
One ear had dropped askew beside one eye
that rolled askew. "It's got into his brain.
Don't treat him rough or he'll go into convulsions,"
the veterinarian said, jabbing him with a needle.

Riding home in the truck the lamb stood gamely
as though facing down a ring of predators,
but he fell when the truck jittered over a pothole
and could not rise. We laid him in a stall
on a mattress of hay, watching him sink and groan
in spite of every attention. We poured water
down his soft throat from a Barbaresco bottle,
stuffed him with purges to push through the poison
that he had gobbled somewhere in the field.
We listened like nurses to his gurgled breath,
laying hands on his hot shaggy flanks, wondering
whether we had left anything undone
we might have done, aghast at being "fastened to
a dying animal." We had no gift
to heal the staggered lamb who had used himself
to help us even out a straggling meadow.
He gave us back his breath in an exchange
for what the meadow gave him, sprigs of laurel
that had lurked deadly in the undergrowth
and plucked his tongue, his brain, among the roses.

BARN FEVER

Nobody knows how much to make of barns,
certainly not a barn as old as this,
set in a farm too swampy and too rocky
to make you rich by cutting hay or grazing.
Our barn was built two hundred years ago—
the lower half. The beams are as old as that.
It probably held harness, kept a horse,
provided cover for a wagon or a pung
and, with boards laid across its crooked roofbeams,
gave half its upper spaces up to hay.
That was before the old house tumbled down
late in the eighteen-fifties. Its next owner,
Malachi* Andrews, who was much involved
in swapping land, begetting farmer's children,
or buying boats for sons who'd rather fish,
rebuilt the barn and then the house and buildings.

That was the golden age of barns. Three farms
were merged by Malachi into a hundred acres
of upland, stoneland, woodland, all to pasture,
mostly for cows. The new half of the barn
stood high enough for storing up salt hay
and sheltering ten milk cows underneath
in wooden stalls so expertly designed,
fitted and whitewashed, that the cow's manure
could be scraped out, without shifting a hoof,
to flow into a cave in the foundations.
The new house, proportioned like the new barn,
rested on masonry as crisp and solid
as the barn's own blocks of fitted Cape Ann stone.
Next to the barn old Malachi then built,
on slender granite pillars that held it off

* pronounced "Mellicky"

the ground, a corncrib with dovetailed corners,
and, near the house, a root cellar and milkshed
to keep the milk and fresh churned butter cool.

For fifty years the barn stood at the center
of the traffic of the farm, above the house
to screen it from the wind. Malachi Andrews,
his offspring scattering from Essex to Salem,
kept up his walls to keep his cows from scattering,
bought lots for firewood, orchard, maple sugar,
and drove to Gloucester every market day.
At night the cows swallowed their cud in the barn.
When Malachi died Elizabeth soon followed.
Their sons went off to sea or to New Jersey,
and two of his daughters, one of them once married,
kept up the barn for two cows and some hens
with only twelve acres left them of the hundred.
They hired a man to help them cut their hay
in the salt marsh and float it up by dory.
They let the sparse old pastureland revert
to meadow. Crab apple and swamp maple
began to creep into the fields which once
had been held open by the force of farming.
One day the two old women, clearing brush,
started a fire to burn the slash, and one,
Miss Mary Brown, was not quite quick enough
to keep her long skirt out of the teeth of the flames
which caught her, brought her down. Her sister
lived on in the house a while but sold the cows.

In the thirty years that passed before I came
trees nudged in and advanced upon the barn.
The corncrib rotted and fell, the milk shed collapsed.
The hayloft in the barn, no longer needed
to keep the cattle fed, was subdivided

9

by two flimsy floors and turned into
a battery for hens, and the cattle stanchions
were strung with chicken wire. No repairs.
Two years more, and the chicken farmer's busted.

The house passed to a Harvard anthropologist
who built himself bookcases in a parlor
that up to then had been reserved for funerals.
He fitted out the kitchen with an electric stove,
dug in new plants around the house, and set
his mind to keeping up a large green lawn—
sure sign that the barn had now become
poor second to a house that was no more a farmhouse.
The anthropologist who tamed the grass
decided the country had become too tame
and sold the farmland to a State Street lawyer
who feared the devastation that would come
if some bad bolshevik laid nuclear waste to Boston.
His wife wallpapered in anticipation.

My first view of the farm: a day in March,
walking with friends down the field between dry stalks.
The barn's soaked black with last night's rain. Its south
wall gapes black with apertures, its eaves are piebald
with doors of nests for squirrels. The high roof,
shingled with asphalt by the chicken farmer,
has lost a number of its links, as though
the wind had tried to scale it like a fish.
Inside, someone's Mercedes. On a beam
two cooing pigeons have scuffled together
a shaggy nest in case of warmer times
for breeding, hatching. All around the barn
sumac and other thicketry are shoving
against the base of the walls, as though to nudge
the ancient building off its pins. The barn

has no friends left, it seems. Some boys have smashed
the floorboards upstairs where the chickens roosted.
If I'm to own it, how to heal the barn?

The house had been infected by the suburbs.
I heard the barn beside it heave a sigh
anticipating usufruct; or else decline,
decay, a sagging and senility;
or, worse, more merciless, a careless match
to send it up in flames like Mary Brown.
Nobody knows how much to make of barns
that do not shelter anything we value.
The crops are spent that went to Haskell's Mill.
This land has turned too sour even for hay
and lies now unprotected by the walls
that run and stumble, madmen, through the woods
which no one cuts or culls. Why are our barns,
that do not shelter anything we value,
left standing as an emblem of a past
when we owned things we thought more worth the keeping?
Sometimes in summertime our younger children
may hide and seek here to remember games
their great-grandparents used to play in barns—
but Malachi and Mary Brown did more than play.
They metamorphosed grass into milk and butter,
kernels and clamshells into hens and eggs,
dead seeds into the brightness of beans and corn.
Somehow the barn is all that they have left us.
What else is lingering on the land to press
its bristling, fading harvests in our arms?
The smells of milk, manure, and straw, a life
beyond the games suburban children play?
Time and some care have spared this barn, a sign
of the work a farm does to keep itself a farm.
Without the barn there would be little cause

to call this piece of land more than a piece
of land, one corner of it fastened down
by a yellow house where people sit and write
about the days when the farm had farmers on it
as well as the busiest barn for miles around.

SATAN IN GOATSKIN

Disarmed on the unhandy
side of the wall, I note
the stern end of the goat
whose forward mouth rips off
my unpicked brussels sprouts.
Lobbed rocks, berserker shouts
shock a stark staring goat into
thick-bodied parody of deer
with grace abounding
to vault and clear
the fence. After which Nanny,
mistress of double-agentry,
bowing, browsing,
shifts shape from pestered
fugitive to pastured
livestock, safely sealed in by wire
with sheep unsafely grazing.
O goat, teetering
on manly hindquarters!
Mount up upon that rock!
O nibble, happy and murderous,
sweet sprigs of apple.
O girdle the boughs.
O kill the tree forever.
O ass-end to our house,
flip up your tail
like the flap of a pocket
and salute the master
who fenced you in his pasture.

FAWN

(for Sam and Jessica Warren)

Late summer dusk. Headlights along the road.
A sudden apparition by the hedge.
My car swerved aside of its own wish,
an instep arch crushed on the brake pedal,
and stopped in an instant. Jumped out
to learn whether we had killed anything
without a sound or click of contact.
Lying on asphalt, dazed but conscious,
half lay a spotted fawn, so scrawny that
I could not tell whether it had been struck
by hunger, illness, or accident. Over one eye
a slight cut, slightly bleeding. The fawn
blinked, lay still. Now other cars were halting.
Occupants were out, shouting advice.
The fawn reclined, dreamy and indifferent.
After a quarter hour of altercation
we heaved the passive, lally-legged baby
into a van, one of us holding a head
that did not need the holding, wary of
the hooves that did not move or strike,
and settled it inside a neighbor's barn
with a sheep-nipple, evaporated milk,
chlorate of lime, a bottle, barley-sugar.
Out of all these warm deer-milk was concocted
and fed into the fawn with deep resistance
from one so weak, so wild, so uncomplaining.
Blowing into the corner of her mouth
triggered a reflex that would make her suckle
and take enough to help her stay alive:
most of the milk ran down along her neck
but some was kept. She lay with folded legs

unmoving, making no attempt to rise
when her feeders approached, not attempting
to give more than a sniff of cooperation.
The second day we took her from the barn
and fed her on the lawn. Her keeper let her go,
and suddenly she found her feet, making for open
country, so weak she could not navigate,
staggering sideways, legs scissoring.
Now, when we tried to put her in the barn,
she flailed out at us with those edged hooves
and struggled till we feared not for ourselves
but her, that she might shatter against the wall.
The third and fourth days she was so much stronger
that her tail flicked up and down when she fed,
and she clattered back and forth in the dark stall.
We took her carefully into the sun,
fed her one last bottle, stood up and back,
and let her go. She walked, mincing forward,
then broke into a trot, and as we watched
she cantered down the lawn and onto the marsh,
tail held high, then out of view into the alders
that border on the marsh. There is no knowing
if she survived the winter, but it was a mild one.

II

THE SOUND OF WINGS

Gift: Some quality or endowment given to man by God or a deity. *Webster*

JULY MEETING

Crow hollered, barking darkness like a trumpet.
Mockingbird followed, dragging behind
a ragbag of moonlit virtuosity.
Robin, at the shank end of mating season,
purled and knit the customary declarations.
Other "feathered songsters" waited,
treading air to hold position
till the loudest at length stood aside.
The cardinal's whistle faded.
Dawn song broke down
into twitter of sparrow and wren,
dove's coo, the receding
ball-peen strokes of oven-bird,
catbird's stuttering clauses.
Finally, after each
had said his grey say,
sun sprang from the edge of sky
into a vacuum of sound,
rewarding every ruddy tree,
calling the world to order.

THATCH

(Spartina alterniflora)

Thatch uncrouches
from the thick brown mat
of marsh like stubble
from the planet's beard,
edges to the seaward side
of its self-humbling cousin
spartina patens,
flourishes seeds overhead
at blade's length, and
flicks them free
into a tide as salt as tears.

PARADISE AS A GARDEN

(for Elizabeth B. Moynihan)

One of the great tautologies: self-regarding:
in which the seeds of growth
are the kernels of contemplation,
in which the contemplation of desire
ekes out desire's last sigh,
in which what enlarges the space
is its surrounding hedges:
husk and flower are one.

These were no northern sprawls, however,
no meadows of bluets and flax.
In Persia water collected itself, at whatever
cost, within walls: model of a house or city:
no water, no life. Yet sometimes paradise
persisted as boundaries only, and in the end
the garden stood, bracelets of stone and water,
without leaf, flower, or fruit to carry temptation.

And so it follows, through ages, crosses and tongues,
that when we speak of our eternal delight,
whether a garden we were once expelled from
or one that has been lost and overgrown,
it is the edges we cannot forget.
Whatever persists within, forever fresh,
is the indelible border of imagination.

THE SOUND OF WINGS

1. *Present Air*

Snow falls off the roof with the sound of wings.
The clouds scud west to east across the sky.
Black birds, my life, starlings, jays and crows,
perch in the tapered boughs of silver trees
waiting for something to live or die. With wings
they barter inklings of life among themselves.

2. *Imperfect Water*

The tide creek fell the way the sun was climbing:
two hours of height until the tide struck low,
two hours till noon. Four hours since snow stopped feeding
the waters while they turned. Their latest high mark smeared
mud-brown against the crystal sheet of snow
while last year's fallen, near-forgotten grasses,
green all washed out by scores of scouring tides,
glared upward, ochre staining sea and sky.

3. *Perfect Fire*

The trees endowed us with this woodpile. Cherry, pear,
maple, and oak (with now and then a whiff
of cedar) have unlimbered, tottered,
and tumbled to the music of the saw,
have stacked their jackstraw limbs beside the barn,
mislaid their growth, fumbled their sap. Thus all
disordered fiber has been realigned
till flame shall filter out the hard from soft
and breathe its distillation to the air.

4. *Future Earth*

This will have been the season's virgin snow,
erasing every blemish, every landmark,
magnifying the earth and all therein
    while it shall continue.

Whether the sun will singe its lap-robe white
or water strip it naked to the air
or wind tuck snow high up against its shoulder,
    it will surely continue.

Its trees will spill their burdens to the wind
and tides will shear off fragments for the sea:
yet snow falls off the roof with the sound of wings
    and it shall continue.

ELSEWHERE IN COLORADO

A world elsewhere? Such dreams are commissars,
calling me to order at meetings, dressing me up
for parties I haven't been invited to,
involving me in love affairs with the Secretary
of Commerce and other unsuitable women (couldn't we
simply be friends?) and assigning me to posts
I haven't volunteered for, elsewhere in Colorado.
Dreams take orders from a parched imagination,
manipulating family and friends like checkers,
contemptuous when I arrive in pinstripe suit
at yet another advertising "presentation,"
or smirking as I attempt to tee off, dufferlike,
on the most intractable of golf courses.
Why do they elect a man of my stripe to walk
through fixes like these, having always to pack
at a moment's notice, change clothes in airplanes,
stumble to table with shoelaces untied?
Yet, when I sit at dinner, grinning across
at a new partner, white-toothed, white-breasted,
I glimpse behind the fluttering gauze at a window
an oriole blazing orange, high in an elm.
He leaps aloft with the hiss of a thrown stone.

ATMOSPHERES

1. *Boulder 1935*

Where the mountains lift from the plain
one boyhood was toughened
in a stucco house, protected
by a palisade of lilacs,
purple one day in April,
the next bowed down in snow
that, melting, would uncover
red slate sidewalks
scribbled over with demotic
marks from children's rollerskates.

The snowflake came and went
in sparse Colorado air
that cracked the boards of pianos,
cooked eggs in cool water,
lifted cakes crankily,
stole away breath at hilltops,
and blotted stray moisture.

Oases? In one direction
the damp innards of Hanselman's
Greenhouse flaunted rainfall
orchids dangling from their roots.
In the other, the English throwback
of Mabel Reynolds' garden.
She ruled it, ramrod straight,
enunciating consonants like musketry
to repel the elisions of the West,
while her husband, Shakespearian George,
smiled on the world as though it were a theatre.

25

The surfaced streets held hard.
Air sizzled in the lungs.
Rocks and gravel abraded
a boy's bare knees despite
the vapors of campus life,
the cries of football crowds
that cheered for Whizzer White,
the oohs and aahs of tourists
at how the falling light
carved shadows in the cliffs
that westward and high upward
clamped down an early sunset
on days that seldom darkened
except with stormclouds or dust
that blew west from the poisoned plains.

2. Cheyenne Mountain 1944

Ten boys of sixteen roped up
on a red crumbling cliff,
guided by a trigonometry teacher.
Climbing boots scuffed the rock,
catching enough edge to heave
bodies over the lip
of a squat ledge, each of us
breathing deep catches of air.
There! Stopped. There, there!
Above, just above. Clear eyes,
moonlit glass, nostrilly head
carrying a sweeping spiral
of horn — stock still, steady
as the rock whose arm he stood on,
a wild ram, bighorn!
Motion and sound both ceased.
When breathing again began
and with a sudden snort,
one of the boys snatched up
his geologist's pick. On wire thighs
he charged the ram. Who blinked,
breathed himself across the outcrops,
seesawed silently upward
and was inhaled by the landscape.
Our pursuer had to halt,
blinking through fogged glasses.
Now decades later, Gifford is dead,
and only a cramped gathering of bighorns
camps, above timberline.

3. National Center for Atmospheric Research, 1967

The fortieth parallel flies around the world
as though launched from the ramparts
of I.M. Pei's mind-fortress. My first guide
to the site, an ancient mathematician,
limped through portals whose lintels
of ground-up mountain stone
glittered slightly with mica.
Below the mesa where the Center stands,
down there in the little city of the plain
where my flesh had flowered for women,
the air drooped thick with pollutants.
The old mathematician croaked out the terrible force
of the geometric progression. "There is no escape.
Population expands, stark as compound interest.
A penny invested by Caesar at simple interest
would be worth a few thousand today; but a penny
at compound interest earns gold
as massive as the planet."
Ieoh Ming's palatial Chinese puzzle
sprouts from the flank of the foothill
like a dusty mushroom. Doorways shackle
vistas of the plains, unimpeded sights
of the sky, green-robed, pink-tinted mountains.
Glass in the windows is tinted
just enough to admit
all elements of the light except glare,
brilliance without dazzle.
Under the molded cover of the walls
unearthly silicon chips,
linked into computer circuits,
monitor the winds of the world
while at their side sit men and women
lightly breathing. Their house

of inquiry shelters without surprise
the earth's commotion, while
the chinook breathes warmly
on dissolving snow.

4. *Boulder 1979*

Where the mountains lift from the plain
I work beside a woman
in kerchief and rounded apron.
We extricate earthenware
from the racks of her kiln.
Her dishes, once moist clay,
now cool and hard as agate,
open their rough-scalloped
rims skyward to swallow
whatever happens to be served
on their surfaces. Flakes of snow
hiss lightly on the glazes
and gather into drops
that the empty air will inhale.

We carry our unfired flesh
through atmospheres and climates
that wait for our decay,
expecting things alive
to take on the life of things.
Change drifts down on our heads
from a past mediated
by mason, shaman, priest—
all those who learned the secret
that the seed must be buried to live,
caught up in atmospheres,
loosening into vapor,
tightening into snowflake.

IL SE SAUVE

*"He saw that he had lost his fear of falling
and all other fears of that nature."*—*John Cheever*

More like a well than a dungeon,
more like a cave than a jail,
the cell shows shadow figures on its wall.
Can such semblances of truth keep
men captive closer
than whip-wielding mistresses
and swag-belted sheriffs? The convicted
tumble into their own preparations—
punjjis, nooses, petards.
Every teaspoon of punishment has been anticipated.

Saints and prisoners embrace such exercises as
pushups, double-entry computations,
mnemonics, and other apportionments.
They write about pilgrims, knights-errant,
victims of illusion. All they need
to expose the vast illusion of prisons
is the wings of an angel.

Even a peregrine's flight may be bribed.
A falconer deceives his hawk with a hood
to which she surrenders in an orderly sequence
of decisions, becoming accustomed
to jesses, gantlets, darkness,
gobbets of dead meat,
rations of light and flight.
The falcon, no angel,
chooses to submit.

The cell itself becomes the enemy.
To accept the minimum security of life,
wings must fall from the shoulders.
Among shadows and sentences you remember
when you could have made a break for it,
when, if you had had the wings of an angel,
you could have got out of here,
uplifted, saved yourself.

III

MEN WORKING

Gift: Something given to corrupt. A bribe.

Oxford

THE SWORDLESS STATUE

(Thomas Ball's "Washington," Boston Public Garden)

A starling sits on the general's hat.
  No sword adorns the empty hand,
yet Washington glares at our hotel
  without surrendering command.

Sculptors and metallists many times
  have filled his hand with substitute steel
to animate the great parade.
  We sit at the Ritz, toy with a meal,

and contemplate how lights illume
  the verdigris Virginian's force,
his garnished grip. Yet knees and thighs
  and reins will hardly urge a horse

if stallion nostrils snort no steam,
  if balls hang green and bare,
if any child can steal a sword
  from the general, riding there.

SHORT WEIGHT

The public scribe measured his life
on a thirty-year lease,
weighing it out in portions
for the use of anyone
who might find it useful.
Peasants came in tears to ask him
to write their letters,
spell out their alliances and contracts,
appreciate the virtue of their motives.
They paid a little. Sometimes he made
a match or made them a market.
Often he supplied written words
they could call their own.
He supported the people and vice versa.

Tuesday at the market some could read
a sign: CLOSED. PERSONAL BUSINESS.
After thirty years! What now?
Will Marie ever learn what became
of her lovely offer of love?
Will Emmanuel's will be proved?
And what of John's plan to plant
a crop of buckwheat beyond the canal?

The moneylenders have had to send away
for a new scribe to explicate
the movements of money, to mediate
the beggar's cry, to brush off
smudge fingers plucking at the sleeve.
The booth will be taken over
by someone hawking lettuce or tortillas,
but the newly-hired maven
of bargain and palaver

will furnish all the words
that send our lives to market,
customers of the country.

THREE MIDRASHIM

1. *Where the Sun Ends* (*Isaiah* 6:8)
   "Eastward I go by force; but westward I go free."
   —*Thoreau: "Walking"*

Mount. Leave your living to the wise.
    Peel out, the highway's for the sun.
Your eyes have pierced the state's disguise,
    Your journey has begun.

Shun shelter, offices, the maze
    of striving. Genitals tell you true:
children sing sweeter praise
    than senators do.

What held you to the empty day,
    the churlish functionary grind
Where unclean lips beseech and bray
    their sermons for the blind?

"A hissing tongue, a shuddering door,"
    the prophets tell, the thrones attest.
Our hoarsened hymns ignite and roar,
    our engines growl toward the West:

    Here am I; send me.

2. *Untuned String* (Psalm 90)

"Yea, the work of our hands, establish thou it."

My childhood Steinway spoke in tongues,
Liebesleid for Schumann,
Lacrimae rerum for Chopin,
hesitant *ostinato* for Purcell,
hypotaxis between the voices of Bach.

Of course, it matters who mans the keyboard.
Sometimes a visitor—Lhevinne, Sykes, Raieff—
could make the family instrument talk turkey,
but when I perched up tight between its legs
my stubby fingers whacked out sounds
that broke the bright charge of music.

O god in the machine! You have cast
a penumbra of sound across all memory,
the purple garment of Europe I wear,
my American secret. And you strike
an even darker note: something's amiss with my hands.
I can carry a tune only with voices.
Never fit to manage
the nineteenth century's noblest invention
(the one that enabled mere men
to establish the work of their hands),
I am shut out from taking a hand in sonatas,
dismissed from polonaise, mazurka, prelude, fugue,
mordant, glissando, thoroughbass.
I may not harrow music with my hands.
I'm struck dumb by a pentecost of piano.

3. *Darkheart* (*Job* 19:26)

The scientist of the night
and the walker in the city
convey me, one at each elbow,
over the shadows of anger
toward my unwillingness.

Wakeful and stiff,
I glower in the darkness
with eyes that will not aid
my body to seek the light.

How graceless to deny
that grunt of understanding:
that only *in my flesh*
shall I see God!

THE TRANSVESTITE'S DREAM

Moving in darkness, under darkened trees,
a figure like a woman, all in black, with long
black hair, sashays through light that glitters
from the last bar open on the avenue.
The impulse roves along abandoned streets
of a city that has nearly stopped its throbbing
and lies asleep (at any rate abed)
for miles around the boulevard where this walker
clicks in spike heels among the trunks of pines.
Moving toward desire, the pulse
of expectation quickens. How could so rare
a creature consent to give in to strangerly darkness?
The footsteps slow, anticipating—what?—
until the eyes flash up appraisingly,
glittering atop a body supple and curved,
canny as a cat. Legs keep strutting.
I yearn to slow down, stop, turn back, to hear
some soft reply, to meet those eyes again.
I halt. Painfully I turn about
and see that waist, the shadowed face averted,
and hear that voice hum, rumbling, *basso buffo.*

LIFE WORK

My father never forgave
himself for the accident
of starting out of wedlock
and took the matter hard,
poisoned by that secret
for the best part of a lifetime.
What hand could he have taken
in the matter, what intervention?
Should he, no matter, have
revolted, interposed
his not-yet-engendered self
between the egg's great moon
and her lathering spermatozoa?
Or, come to term at length,
wasted himself on sluts,
furrowed himself with drink,
and, *schrecklich,* blown apart
the lid of his head?

Since change has more to do
with life than even life,
the waste of shame is this:
that shame sticks at prevention:
it keeps earth off, water level,
air out, fire away,
away from the nameless self,
away from the staring world.

THE LAUGHTER OF WOMEN

When men go out for laughs, they go all out,
baring their teeth, betraying no memory
of the slave quarters, master's rumpled bed,
heaps of hacked corpses at the river crossing,
bodies bent back in alleyways or gardens.
Men's voices rise and sharpen nasally
to slice even their brothers off at the knees,
ho-hoing at the gallons of booze, the babes
the other put away the night before.
"Hey Roy, better shut your eyes
before you bleed to death."

The laughter of women holds half a world at bay,
whether the giggles of girls leering askance
at the hulking narcissistic strut of an athlete,
or the hushed laughter of a fiancée
feeling the stranger's eyes upon her breasts,
or the stylized *ha-ha* of zarzuela dancers
(hand on one hip, flower in the teeth,
wrist flung overhead like a whiplash).
Laughter gives women strength, protection, help:
men wonder just how safe their secret is.

"We know your ways," men hear that laughter say.
"Women have bathed and dressed boy babies, and
we cannot disremember what you are.
Though we sway to your sex, what woman has no fear
that love will promptly turn away its face
the day she trusts you to implant a life?
To make light of man's yoke, that costly burden,
we laugh at the dark, the dark that pulls us down."

The laughter of a woman is her pride.
Men smile and shake their heads to think of it,
how gladly women wear our rings, our houses.
The heads of women lean together, laughing.

IV

MIXED BLESSINGS

Gift: (German) Poison, toxin, virus, venom;
virulence, malice, fury. (*Cassell's German
Dictionary*)

Gift: (Swedish) Marriage

SLEEPING BEAUTY VARIATIONS

(for Peter Shaffer)

Marriage or poison. Which was the gift
   that struck princes limp at the castle wall
like stones become too heavy to lift?

Matchmakers smirked, courtiers sniffed,
   godmother grinned from the head of the hall.
Marriage or poison, which was the gift?

Supple Aurora, maiden adrift,
   sheds blood, turns woman and takes the fall,
stone become too heavy to lift.

The world knows ways to give short shrift
   to sex that smothers itself in a pall
of marriage or poison. Which *was* the gift?

Upstairs the sleepers stir and shift.
   Time trickles down to bury us all,
stones become too heavy to lift.

The race we know is not to the swift.
   Slow sleeps out his life in a stall.
   Marriage or poison, which was the gift?
The stone become too heavy to lift?

JANUARY 1977

You had "never been absent." The nation hissed
    with blizzards. Telephone rang:
your voice from Tulsa. My heart and tongue
    interfered to say no more than
        "I miss you,"

blotting out news of white skies that had frozen
    sheep dead where they stood,
news of the illnesses of children. My love
    for your body skated across
a continent chilled to its heart with low temperatures
    setting new records.

Your voice had faded. Dreams reinforced
    the remoteness: I'm shut from our house,
from your bed, kneeling bareshins in slush.
    Dream islands breed
poisoned shellfish, dream bridges
    won't reach. My hands
tingled to cup your breasts but shut
    as cold as the plains.

NEW YEAR'S EVE

The club is filling, tables draped with linen.
Behind the scenes waiters open wine.
Early arrivals are already tabled in corners.
I scurry to a bathroom to cover up, for
a ceremony is in the making. I cannot qualify
until I'm dressed in stiff shirt, shiny shoes,
black tie wrestled by trembling fingers,
jacket with shiny lapels.
The more I dress, the more I'm like the others;
the more I dress, the more invisible;
the more I dress, the more alone.

Now, seated at the rout, right hand around a glass
of clearest gin, I nod and smile at the penguins.
Soon—another sip of gin—
the door will swing wide and admit, from the outside dark,
spectres of the women I have loved.
Here's the head of one, the breasts of another, the silky
hair of a third, the perfume of a fourth,
the wetness of another long forgotten.

I stand and watch the broad one, the tall one, the small one.
Before my eyes they merge into one woman.
I'd have one girl take all the flaming decades
and burn them to cinders with her clear blue eyes.

ON ITHACA

Settling at home, after Calypso, Circe
and Nausicaa, in Penelope's olive-tree bed,
among flocks of sheep and swine, surrounded by orchards,
how will Odysseus die? Will Penelope fuck him to death?
Or will he take to drinking with the swineherds?
In a pool Odysseus regards his body, comely
as when the women bathed it, and Athene
touched it with ambrosia till it glowed.
Later, abed, he dreams of Polyphemus,
the red-hot stake, the shriek, the sizzling eyeball,
that other flock of sheep, the great ram for escape,
the suitors feasting in the high-roofed hall,
the gouts of blood that spurted from his arrows.

WORDLESS WINTER

1. *Clinical Depression*

who cares what name you call it   here it comes
curling around the house in the dark like mist
that has no dampness   settling on my chest
like a weightless bird   tell it to go away
shout   clap your hands   let them stare
this visitor has no parents   where it lives
when it isnt invading innocent islands
I cannot guess for the life of me   I guess
it must have habitation in my cells
imprisoned like a foaming lunatic   shaking
the bars of my body   keeping the entire penitentiary
awake   baying me moonward night after night

who has seen low pressure   neither you nor I
but to deny the fact of my possession by it
is to declare myself swept clean of devils
and weep   goodbye depression   hello anxiety

2. The Clinic

When you say, "You haven't
done anything wrong," you must mean
that if I had done it, it could not
be wrong, being my act.

Such high regard the doctor
professes for the patient! That my most
ravenous desire should be characterized
as innocently as a pail of milk,
or one leg dreamily thrown over another!

Could you have meant that all sins
are equal, that there's "nothing
abnormal" in such behavior?

Then fact steps up with more
than moral news: *We found
cancer cells on the slide.*

You declare, "You haven't done
anything wrong." And I reply,
    "Haven't I?"

3. *Willing Her to Live*

O, she's dying all right. But maybe
no faster than anyone else,
as Mark Twain said in response
to certain inquiries.
Among the remnants of a harvest,
sweating and staring in my garden,
I shovel dark infusions of manure
across pale autumn soil
in layers of enriching history,
stuff that cattle had devoured,
chewed over, passed through
before keeping a date with the butcher.

As I excite topsoil for next year
I wonder who will eat what's not yet grown
or whether anyone will plant it.
Wetly, blindly I keep shovelling.
Earth snatches compost back
like a transfusion and will not pause
to keep a leaf attached
in response to prayers or tears
or the use of shovels.

4. *Frozen Drought*

Surprising sunshine has ruled more than a hundred days
of this bare winter. Snow has forgotten itself.
The ground lies hard as stone and flat with dust
as though the surface were peeling in the wind
and blowing off to hell or to dust-heaven.
Neighbors and newspapers speak of the oddity,
snowless New England! Week after week blows by
and the ground grows dryer and the teeth grit.
The nose seals up against an invasion
of drought in Eastern air that never tasted
the brown dark of the dust over bleeding Kansas.

5. *Householder*

What can explain this ebb-tide of emotion,
this failure of joints and parts,
this position, as intolerable as
a turned turtle?
Hand will not clench on its pen,
head mislays its calling.
Heart? Content to keep beating.

This unfever has its blessings:
the bleaching out of anger.
A sensibility confined
to the predictable.
Indoor plants, domesticated animals.
No wild birds, no wild weather.
An implacable appetite
for things as they are. A nice gratitude
for the unresisted passage of time.

As householder I have felt
entitled to hope for better.
Now I pray to keep out of bed,
ask for no worse.
My friends hear nothing from me
once highly regarded, nor
do my enemies.
I have been taught by mixed blessings,
poisoned apples,
to sit apart, muscles clenched like marble.

6. *Stalemate*

Her will has worked
to the surface,
outcarving that smooth
genetic chisel that incised
rills running
like inlets toward
her cornflower-blue eyes.
I kiss their corners.

Whatever it is that keeps
her harnessed
to the burden of her body
has impressed a set
of stretch marks on the forehead
like reinforcements.

Her face, a landscape, carries
the colors of contending forces:
a tug of joy, eyes lit with laughter;
a nagging hermit mask;
a cloud of pain.

7. *After Winter Slaughtering*

Our pigs have spent weeks away from their pen,
but hoofprints frozen in midnight mud
remember in ice the shape of a thigh
that, slaughtered, severed, relieved of blood,
lies cold in the dark as a blinded eye
counting lineup shots of arrested men.

8. *The Writing Lesson*

Miss Daisy M. Johnston enforced her rules:
no wiggling, talking, or gum.
Hands clasped, or flat on the desk,
never out of sight in the lap.

Miss Daisy gospelled the Palmer Method:
write, write, write with the arm, not with the fingers;
push and pull as though conducting music.
The pencil must be held airily, unsqueezed,
guided through wrist, thumb and elbow,
mastered by the shoulder,
guided by the waist.

Who, learning letters in this fashion,
could reserve adequate breath
to shriek for help
when muscles clenched in complaint
and the center of the body disclaimed them
and the poet, hands flat on the desk,
no wiggling, talking, or gum,
felt the dark cadence castigate his arm?

MY LADY THE LAKE

It is the lake within the lake that drowns.
Sunbeams gnaw into its dark, never again
to be released as light. The lake swallows
whatever it is fed. It eats its ice each spring,
nibbles for years at fallen twigs and timber,
engorges the heat of summer with each sunset,
closes around corpse of dragonfly and beaver.
By its waters I have sat down and wept, without
taking any comfort or return
except for the offer of what it has translated:
frogs, crayfish, sticklebacks. The trout
stocked by a prescient owner crammed themselves,
after the passage of several seasons, up
against its banks to die. It devoured their bones.
Still water gives us only a reflection.
Whatever we cast in, it will accept,
and in such lakes within the lake we drown.

Peter Davison must be one of the very few American poets of his generation never to have either studied or taught creative writing. The son of the poet Edward Davison, he was encouraged in his youth by Robert Frost, a family friend, and began in his late twenties to write poems, as described in his autobiography, *Half Remembered*. Dudley Fitts chose his first volume, *The Breaking of the Day*, in 1964 for inclusion in the Yale Series of Younger Poets. He has worked with distinction for three decades as an editor of books, since 1956 at the Atlantic Monthly Press, and he is also poetry editor of *The Atlantic*. He lives, with his wife, the writer Jane Davison, on a farm in Gloucester, Massachusetts, which is the background for many of the poems in *Barn Fever*.